FAMILY
UPPER TE

CW00394112

CONTENTS

WALKS OF DISCOVERY

Middleton-in-Teesdale - Scoberry Bridge - Newbiggin Circular

1 From the Teesdale Hotel turn left, along Market Place, then right, along Bridge Street, crossing the Tees to turn right just past the cattle market at a footpath sign, joining the Pennine Way. Follow a clear track edging two fields, passing an outbuilding on the right and continuing, still on a clear track, soon to edge the Tees along a high embankment, now on a path which soon enters a walled lane.

2 At its end continue along a clear path edging the left side of fields until a Pennine Way signpost directs you along a grassy path down the middle of a field to its far corner from where the path continues, soon to rejoin the river along the rim of a wooded bank.

3 On reaching a yellow arrow on a post, turn right, descending to cross two closely sited streams and reach the riverside. Turn left, upstream, along a clear, stiled path until Scoberry Bridge is reached.

4 Turn right over the bridge and cross the Tees. Go over the field ahead to a facing gate, cross the next field and cross Bow Lee Beck on a footbridge. Follow a walled lane, cross a stile and continue, diagonally right, across the field ahead, leaving over a stile onto the B6277. Turn right, along the road, then left at Rose Cottage Farm, up a lane.

5 Turn right at a T-junction at the Wesleyan chapel, continuing along the road, which, on leaving Newbiggin, bends left, climbing steeply. Leave the road, right, on this bend, into a field.

6 Cross the field diagonally left to leave over a ladder stile in the facing wall. Now go diagonally right over a meadow, climbing towards woodland. On crossing the brow of the hill, a stile in a facing wall comes into view, which you cross. Go diagonally left, guided by a yellow arrow, soon to see a step stile ahead, which you cross into Brockers Gill.

7 Take the path ahead, bearing slightly left, which soon crosses a culvert, then climbs the Gill's far side, which, in springtime is a deep blue carpet of bluebells.

The path ends with a short, steep scramble to join a track, where you turn right along it, briefly, to leave the wood on a ladder stile.

8 Continue along the bottom of the next field, exit through a gap stile to the right of a facing gate and go diagonally left up the steep hillside. As you climb, a stile to the left of a hawthorn comes into view. Cross it and immediately turn right, edging the field and leaving through a facing gate.

9 Cross the next two fields, straight ahead, leaving over right-hand corner stiles. Cross a lane and immediately enter the field ahead over a stile.

10 Edge the field, close to a wall on the right, bearing left, towards its end, to a gate in the middle of a facing wall. Once through it, cross a short field, bearing left to leave over a left-hand corner stile onto the road.

11 Keeping in the same direction, follow the road, which brings you nicely back into Middleton-in-Teesdale.

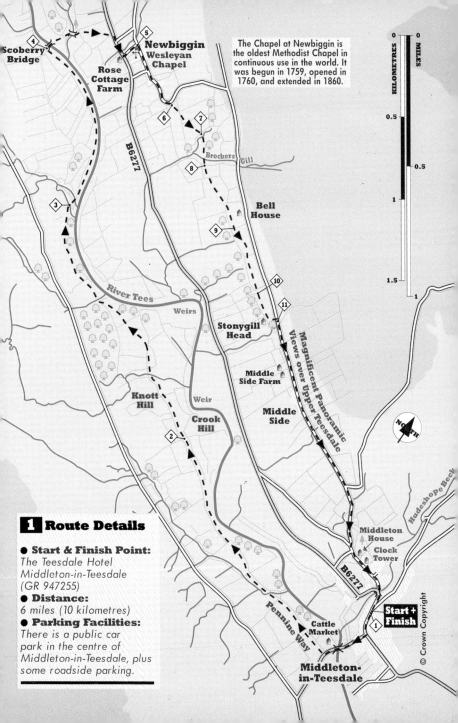

Scoberry
Bridge

④

⑤ **Newbiggin**
Wesleyan
Chapel

Rose
Cottage
Farm

The Chapel at Newbiggin is
the oldest Methodist Chapel in
continuous use in the world. It
was begun in 1759, opened in
1760, and extended in 1860.

⑥

⑦

B6277

Brockers Gill

⑧

③

Bell
House

⑨

River Tees

⑩

Weirs

⑪

Stonygill
Head

Middle
Side Farm

Magnificent Panoramic Views over Upper Teesdale

Knott
Hill

Weir

Middle
Side

Crook
Hill

②

NORTH

Hudeshope Beck

Middleton
House

Clock
Tower

B6277

1 Route Details

● **Start & Finish Point:**
The Teesdale Hotel
Middleton-in-Teesdale
(GR 947255)
● **Distance:**
6 miles (10 kilometres)
● **Parking Facilities:**
There is a public car
park in the centre of
Middleton-in-Teesdale, plus
some roadside parking.

Pennine Way

Cattle
Market

Start +
Finish

①

Middleton-
in-Teesdale

© Crown Copyright

KILOMETRES   MILES

0   0

0.5

0.5

1

1.5

1

Middleton-in-Teesdale - Aukside - Coldberry - Middleside Circular

1 From the Teesdale Hotel cross the road and turn right along the B6277, soon to bridge Hudeshope Beck. Where the B6277 curves left, keep straight ahead, uphill. When almost at the hill's brow, turn right, up a curving flight of steps and go along a path between houses, continuing along a lane, passing houses on the left, and overlooking Hudeshope valley and Middleton on the right.

2 Soon after a house on the left is fronted, the path joins a track. Continue along it through woodland. In a short distance, when the track curves right, bear left, along a climbing path close to the wall on the left. Exit through a wicket gate in the corner of a facing wall and continue along a clear path, curving right, across a field to the left-hand side of a property to cross a facing stile.

3 Cross the next field, diagonally left, to another stile in a facing wall. Continue over the next field, parallel to the wall on the right, to a facing gateway, cross the field ahead diagonally right to exit through a gate partly along the wall on the right, from where you go diagonally left, up the next field, to leave through a gate to the left-hand side of Aukside farmhouse.

4 Cross a short garth to the left of the house and exit through a facing gate. Within a few metres turn right, along a farm road, and short of a facing gate, turn left, through a stile and go up the right-hand side of a wood. Leave over a stile and cross the field ahead, bearing slightly right, aiming for a footpath sign to the left of High Aukside House, ahead.

5 Now turn right, along a minor road, for a mile and, just past Club Gill, bear left to Coldberry Mine along a track, passing first an old reservoir, then a brick building and an adit, a mine entrance, to reach the mine shop, where you turn left.

6 Continue, ascending, to the right of some double walls, past two chimney pots and an old enamelled water trough, roughly parallel to but some distance from Coldberry Gutter, a vast hush. The way is undefined, the direction south-westerly. Coldberry Mine, the largest lead mine in Teesdale, was the last one to close. It remained open until 1955.

7 Go through a gate and, keeping in the same direction, cross a step stile in a fence. As the flank of Hardberry Hill is crossed, go through the middle of three gates, leaving this tussocky common. Now follow a descending path, close to the wall on your left, passing through two gateways, to join a steeply descending, rutted track which meets a tarmac road at a road junction. The narrow Miry Lane ahead descends the very steep hill leading to Newbiggin.

8 However, you turn left here, along the tarmac lane roughly contouring the hillside and stay on it for two pleasant, airy miles, back to the start. As the descent into Middleton is made, Middleton House and the Lead Yard Clock Tower are passed and, all too soon, you are at your destination.

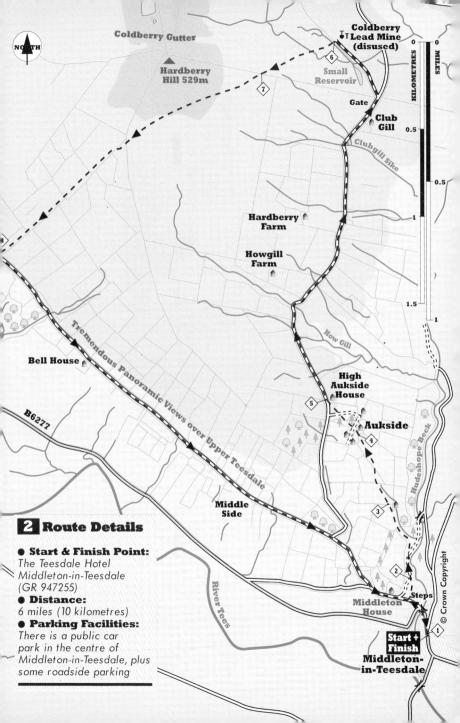

NORTH

Coldberry Gutter

Hardberry
Hill 529m

Coldberry
Lead Mine
(disused)

Small
Reservoir

7

6

Gate

Club
Gill

Clubgill Sike

KILOMETRES | MILES
0 — 0
0.5
0.5
1
1.5
1

Hardberry
Farm

Howgill
Farm

How Gill

Bell House

Tremendous Panoramic Views over Upper Teesdale

High
Aukside
House

5

Aukside

4

Hudeshope Beck

B6277

Middle
Side

3

2

River Tees

Middleton
House

Steps

1

**Start +
Finish**

**Middleton-
in-Teesdale**

© Crown Copyright

2 Route Details

● **Start & Finish Point:**
*The Teesdale Hotel
Middleton-in-Teesdale
(GR 947255)*
● **Distance:**
6 miles (10 kilometres)
● **Parking Facilities:**
*There is a public car
park in the centre of
Middleton-in-Teesdale, plus
some roadside parking*

3 Middleton·in·Teesdale - Kirkcarrion - Bowbank Circular

Kirkcarrion is one of the most prominent landmarks of Upper Teesdale. Approach Middleton from any direction and Kirkcarrion hits you in the eye. Perched high on a knoll, this walled circle of woodland is a splendid sight and simply screams for closer inspection. If that were all, it would be enough; but there is more to Kirkcarrion than meets the eye. It is shrouded in mystery, has an interesting past and the ghosts of the long dead call it home. It is the Bronze Age burial site of the Brigantes Prince Caryn and legend has it that he is responsible for the feeling that unseen eyes are watching your every move and for raising your dog's hackles. Kirkcarrion is private but this excellent wedge shaped walk will bring you within close proximity of its boundary wall.

1 From the Teesdale Hotel turn left, along Market Place, then right, down Bridge Street and over the Tees. On reaching the road junction to Holwick, turn right for a few metres, then left, through an inset gate, signposted, and follow a track up the field ahead leaving through a facing gate.

2 Continue along the track and, where it divides, take the left-hand fork, climbing to cross a stile near a facing gate. Follow the track ahead, which edges towards the wall on the left, reaching it at a gate, on the left, which you go through.

3 Continue along a clear track, which soon divides. Now take the left-hand, lower track, which soon descends. Where this track splits, take the right-hand fork to join the B6276. This part of the walk offers fine views of Lunedale and its two reservoirs, Grassholme and Selset. These reservoirs are very successful fisheries and their Lunedale setting is typical of the Pennine Dales. They are two of Northumbria Water's most popular fisheries with both wild brown and stocked rainbow trout found there.

4 Turn left, along the main B6276 road (being very watchful for and careful of the traffic) to Bowbank hamlet and just before the last house on the left, Low Side Farm, turn left, along a short lane into a field where you turn left and go diagonally right, uphill, along a green track. Where it ends, continue along a contouring path, which could be a sheep trod, and where that ends turn right along a short depression and climb out of it to a rather indistinct stile in a facing wall, slightly left of where, behind the wall, another wall meets it at right angles.

5 Cross the stile and continue up the field ahead close to the wall on the right. On reaching a gate in this wall, go through it and turn diagonally left to cross the field ahead parallel to the wall on the right to exit at a metal stile in an obtuse corner of the facing wall.

6 Descend the rough pasture ahead, close to the wall on the left, and, a little beyond a gate in this wall turn left, over a metal stile set into it.

7 Here go diagonally right, briefly to rejoin the outward route at a tangent and retrace your steps along it, for a pleasant return to Middleton-in-Teesdale.

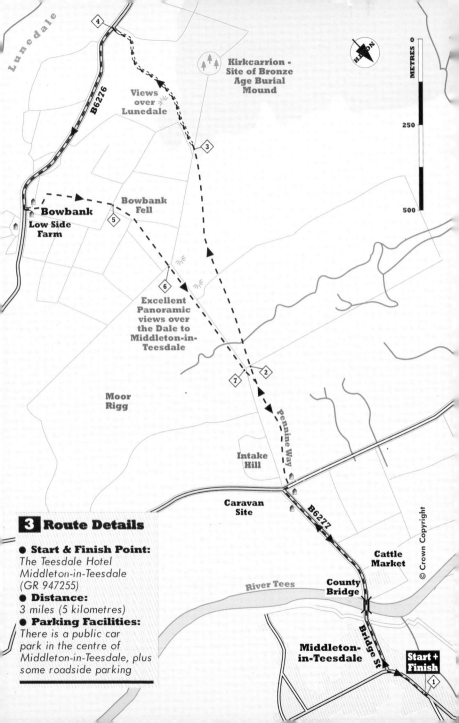

Lunedale

4

B6276

Views over Lunedale

Kirkcarrion - Site of Bronze Age Burial Mound

METRES 0

250

500

3

Bowbank Fell

5

Bowbank

Low Side Farm

6

Excellent Panoramic views over the Dale to Middleton-in-Teesdale

Moor Rigg

7

2

Pennine Way

Intake Hill

Caravan Site

B6277

© Crown Copyright

Cattle Market

3 Route Details

● **Start & Finish Point:**
The Teesdale Hotel Middleton-in-Teesdale (GR 947255)
● **Distance:**
3 miles (5 kilometres)
● **Parking Facilities:**
There is a public car park in the centre of Middleton-in-Teesdale, plus some roadside parking

River Tees

County Bridge

Middleton-in-Teesdale

Bridge St

Start + Finish

1

4 Middleton·in·Teesdale - Snaisgill - Monk's Moor - High Dyke Circular

1 From the Teesdale Hotel turn right, pass the church on the right and take the uphill road. Pass the right turning to Stanhope, keeping straight ahead, along the road signposted 'Snaisgill 1 mile'.

2 When Snaisgill is reached and the road bends sharp left to cross the head of the gill turn right, a few metres past the bend, through a gate at a public footpath sign, onto open grassland. Climb the rough pasture ahead, bearing slightly left to meet the wall on the left at a tangent about mid-way along it where you cross it by a stile sited at a bolt hole in the wall.

3 Keeping in the same direction, climb the hillside, pulling away from the wall, now on your right. Soon a facing wall is seen with, in front of it, a cart track leading to an as yet unseen gate in it. On reaching the cart track, continue along it to go through the now seen facing gate. Curlews are piping and the views are superb. Follow a green track that runs up the middle of the field ahead. Soon a facing wall comes into view; and as soon as you see it, leave the green track, which curves left, to go through a facing step stile onto moorland.

4 Continue, close to the wall on your left, which soon begins to bear slightly left. From here, on the horizon, can be seen a stone shooting butt on the left and a prominent cairn. Go forward, aiming midway between the two, moving away from the wall on your left and climbing. As height is gained, a rusty, corrugated building comes into view beneath a rocky outcrop. Aim to the right of the building, through a line of butts, and climb the outcrop onto Monk's Moor, a flat plateau. From here a large collapsed shelter can be seen at the plateau's northern end. Called Monk's Currick, at 565 metres, it is the highest point on Monk's Moor and the apex of the walk. From it the all round views are superb. Good butty stop!

5 Retrace your steps to the stile leading onto the moor, cross it and immediately turn left, alongside the wall on your left, gradually easing away from it along a narrow path, curving right, but not losing height, towards the woodland at the bottom left-hand corner of the pasture.

6 On reaching the corner, go through a gate in the wall on your left into a ruinous sheepfold, exiting through a gateway. Turn right to face distant Grassholme Reservoir and go diagonally left to a step in a facing wall. Go along the step and through a facing gate, continuing down the right-hand side of a field, speckled yellow with buttercups in early summer, along a green track.

7 Exit at the right-hand corner of a facing wall and go diagonally left over the next field, following a clear track. Go through a gate in a facing fence and continue along the track, leaving the field onto a road.

8 Turn right, along it, to join the outward road at a T-junction, where you turn left, back to the start.

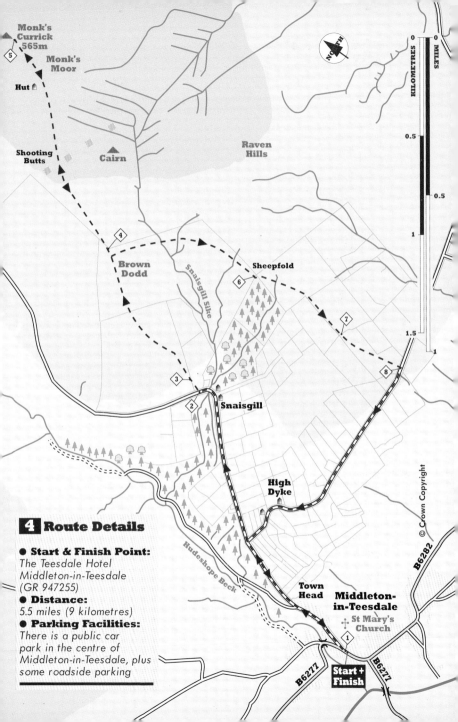

Monk's
Currick
565m
5

Monk's
Moor

Hut 🏠

Shooting
Butts

Cairn

Raven
Hills

4

Brown
Dodd

Snaisgill Sike

Sheepfold

6

7

3

2

Snaisgill

8

High
Dyke

Hudeshope Beck

Town
Head

Middleton-
in-Teesdale

St Mary's
Church

1

Start +
Finish

B6277

B6277

B6282

© Crown Copyright

NORTH

KILOMETRES   MILES

0   0

0.5

0.5

1

1.5

1

4 Route Details

● **Start & Finish Point:**
The Teesdale Hotel
Middleton-in-Teesdale
(GR 947255)
● **Distance:**
5.5 miles (9 kilometres)
● **Parking Facilities:**
There is a public car
park in the centre of
Middleton-in-Teesdale, plus
some roadside parking

Middleton-in-Teesdale - Beck Road - Coldberry - Snaisgill Circular

1 From the Teesdale Hotel turn right, passing the church on the right, and continue uphill, along a tarmac road edged with houses.
2 On leaving Middleton take the first left, through woodland, descending to run alongside Hudeshope Beck, still on a tarmac road.

This pleasant, arboreal route stays alongside the beck for almost a mile before bridging it and losing its surface, continuing, now with the beck on its right, as a rough track for a further third of a mile before ending abruptly at the foot of a very steep, wooded bank.
3 Here bear left, along a path and almost at once turn left over a waymarked stile in a fence on the left and immediately turn right, along a clear path, soon to pass another yellow arrow before climbing the steep bank. At the top of it follow the path between conifers to a facing fence fronting a facing wall. Cross the fence on a stile, immediately turn left for a few metres and turn right to cross the wall on another stile.

Climb the bank in the field ahead, going between two trees, and, on reaching the banks brow, continue straight ahead to cross a stile in a facing wall now clearly seen ahead.

Cross the next field bearing slightly left, leaving over a step stile in a facing wall. Cross the third field, a narrow one, in the same direction, again leaving over a step stile in a facing wall, against which, for guidance, a large slab of stone has been placed.
4 Continue across a rough pasture, following a green path, which becomes clearer as it approaches, then descends Clubgill Sike, which makes a deep gash right down the middle of the field. The path crosses the narrow sike that flows along this depression at a point where a footbridge once spanned it. Now only one buttress remains.

Climb the far side, in the same direction, bearing slightly to the left to go through a gap in some rushes. As the land levels out a stile in a facing wall comes into view. Aim for and cross

it.

From this stile, the retrospective view, southwards, towards Middleton is a particularly fine one.

Continue, bearing diagonally left, passing a white painted building, Club Gill, on the left, to meet the wall on your left at a tangent at a signposted stile.
5 Cross the stile onto a minor tarmac road and continue along it, descending, soon to go through a facing metal gate.

Stay on the road as it passes through an area of despoliation, of the skeletal remains of a long dead lead mining industry. From it can be seen a landscape tormented into unnatural shapes, the result of 'hushing', the flooding away of channels of topsoil to expose the lead ore. In parts grass attempts to soften the effect, but grass cannot work miracles. Yet it is a good example of nature trying to free itself from the ravages of man.
6 The road crosses Hudeshope Beck on a pipe bridge and soon heads south, contouring the valley most pleasantly past Snaisgill to bring you enjoyably, back to the start of the walk.

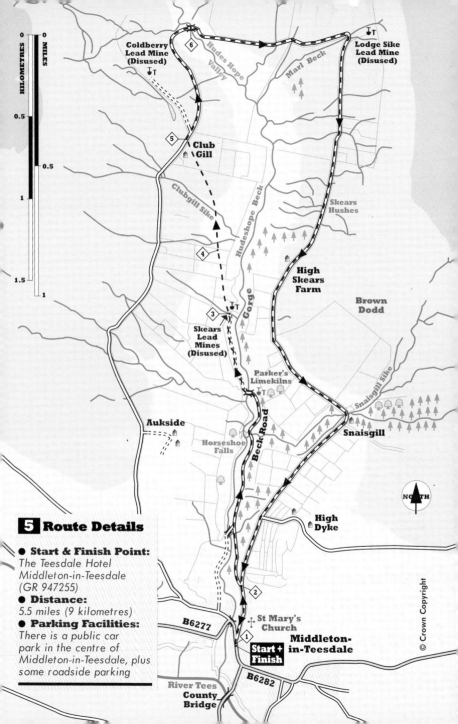

KILOMETRES   MILES

0   0

0.5

0.5

1

1.5

1

Coldberry
Lead Mine
(Disused) T

6

Hudes Hope
Valley

Marl Beck

Lodge Sike
Lead Mine
(Disused) T

5

Club
Gill

Clubgill Sike

Hudeshope Beck

Skears
Hushes

High
Skears
Farm

Brown
Dodd

4

3   T

Skears
Lead
Mines
(Disused)

Gorge

Parker's
Limekilns   T

Snaisgill Sike

Aukside

Horseshoe
Falls

Beck Road

Snaisgill

NORTH

High
Dyke

5 Route Details

● **Start & Finish Point:**
*The Teesdale Hotel
Middleton-in-Teesdale
(GR 947255)*
● **Distance:**
5.5 miles (9 kilometres)
● **Parking Facilities:**
*There is a public car
park in the centre of
Middleton-in-Teesdale, plus
some roadside parking*

2

St Mary's
Church

1

**Start +
Finish**

**Middleton-
in-Teesdale**

B6277

B6282

River Tees
County
Bridge

6 Middleton-in-Teesdale - Leekworth Farm - River Tees Circular

Whereas a Town Trail, like Walk 12, provides an insight into Middleton's manifold attractions, this grand, little circular will enable you to view this sturdy market town in relation to the surrounding countryside; and once you have seen how Middleton not only fits into but actually improves its setting, you are well on the way to being hooked, which can't be bad because it means you would like to make a return visit!

1 From the Teesdale Hotel turn left, along Market Place, continuing eastwards towards that side of town and where the B6282, which runs through it curves left, continue straight ahead, along Leekworth Gardens, between dwellings.

2 The clear path across the fields provides a retrospective look at Middleton, showing how it spreads across a terrace, its solid stone buildings, well-suited to withstand Upper Teesdale's harsh winter weather, being attractive enough to tempt tourists and hikers during the summer months.

3 After ¾ mile, on approaching a little wooded gill, turn right, through a stile in a wall on the right and descend a meadow, leaving over a stile in a facing wall, guided by a 'Teesdale Way' sign.

4 The Teesdale Way is a new long distance footpath, which takes its name from the beautiful river along which it threads. It has as its symbol a dipper, which is prominently displayed on all the Teesdale Way's distinctive, yellow arrows and signposts. Tremendous efforts have been made to make this long distance footpath as accessible as possible and nature ensures that its natural beauty is the valley's crowning glory. Middleton is now further blessed because now two long distance footpaths, the Teesdale Way and the Pennine Way meet there.

Local hotels and bed and breakfast establishments in and around Middleton cater equally enthusiastically both for hikers walking these long distance footpaths and others who are content to restrict their activities to little gems like this one. In fact, in Middleton those who seldom if ever walk are as well catered for as those who do.

The path descends towards a caravan site, on the right, and soon a waymarked stile is crossed, bringing you into the field in which the caravans stand.

5 This caravan site, one of many in Upper Teesdale, reflects, in part, the change that has come about in the dale's industries. Where once lead mining was a principal source of income, today it is farming and tourism. Edge the field, close to the Tees on the left, in flamboyant mood thereabouts, and leave it over a facing stile in the field's left-hand corner.

6 Continue along the riverbank, following a delightful path which becomes flagged as Middleton is edged, all the way to the County Bridge, the latter part being in the steps of the miners of old.

7 Turn right along Bridge Street, and at its end turn left, along Market Place, back to the start.

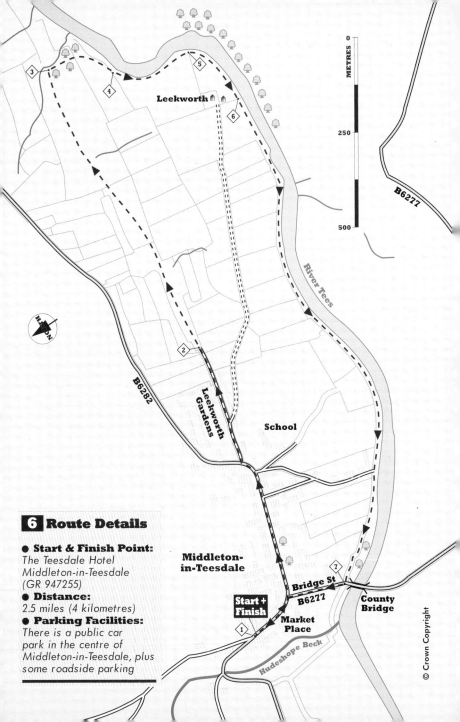

METRES

0

250

500

B6277

River Tees

Leekworth

B6282

Leekworth Gardens

School

Middleton-in-Teesdale

Bridge St
B6277

County Bridge

Start + Finish

Market Place

Hudeshope Beck

6 Route Details

● **Start & Finish Point:**
The Teesdale Hotel
Middleton-in-Teesdale
(GR 947255)
● **Distance:**
2.5 miles (4 kilometres)
● **Parking Facilities:**
There is a public car
park in the centre of
Middleton-in-Teesdale, plus
some roadside parking

© Crown Copyright

7 Middleton-in-Teesdale - Grassholme Reservoir - Harter Fell Circular

1 From the Teesdale Hotel turn left, along Market Place, right along Bridge Street, cross the Tees, turn immediately left, through a waymarked wicket gate, go downstream, soon to follow a farm road to where it enters a farmyard.

2 Follow the riverbank on a rough track that soon curves right. Cross a facing stile. Follow the track ahead, briefly, close to the hedge on your left. At a yellow arrow, bear right, over the field and up a bank, exiting through a facing gap stile. Cross the next field diagonally left to a stile in a wall on the left. Cross the field ahead, at first close to the wall on the left, then pulling away to a clearly seen gate ahead. Exit through a gap stile to the left of the gate, guided by a footpath sign.

3 Turn left, along the road, passing a farm on the right. Turn right at a footpath sign, cross a field at the farm entrance, close to the wall on your right and cross a ladder stile onto a disused railway line.

4 Turn left, along it. Cross Lunedale Viaduct.

Turn right, along a lane to Westfield House, turn left at a footpath sign, edge the field ahead, passing a house on the left, exiting through a facing gateway in its left-hand corner. Cross the next field diagonally right, exiting over a stile at the right-hand corner of a facing fence and descend into a valley.

5 Turn right, through a waymarked gateway, go diagonally left, through a gap stile and continue diagonally right, up the field ahead, guided by yellow arrows. Exit at a stile in the right-hand corner of a facing fence. Climb the rough pasture ahead, cross a facing waymarked fence and continue close to the wall on the right to cross a waymarked stile in it. Continue diagonally left, aiming for a line of middle distance trees. Exit at a signposted stile onto a road.

6 Turn right. Go along it for one mile with Grassholme Reservoir to your right, before turning right to bridge the reservoir. Continue along the road, climbing until the B6276 is reached. Turn right along the road until you

meet the track on the left to Wythes Hill Farm.

7 Follow the track past the farm on your right to reach Carl Beck.

8 Cross the stream, climb a field to its right-hand corner, exiting at a white stile. Cross a rough pasture diagonally left along an undulating path, to a stile on the right. Follow a broad path and, at a cairn, go left, along a farm track, through a gateway. Continue right, as directed, bearing left to a facing gateway, cross the field ahead, then the next one, along a track that curves left, exiting at a facing gate.

9 Cross the field ahead on a clear track to a facing stile. Continue along a clear track through a waymarked gate, then right, to a white stile beyond. Cross the next field. Go through a gateway on your left and down the next field on a clear path to a facing gate.

10 Bear diagonally right along a clear, descending path to a gate in a fence on the left. Beyond it, bear right, over pasture to a facing gate. Descend the field ahead, along a track, to the road.

11 Turn right to the junction, then left, along the B6277, to Middleton.

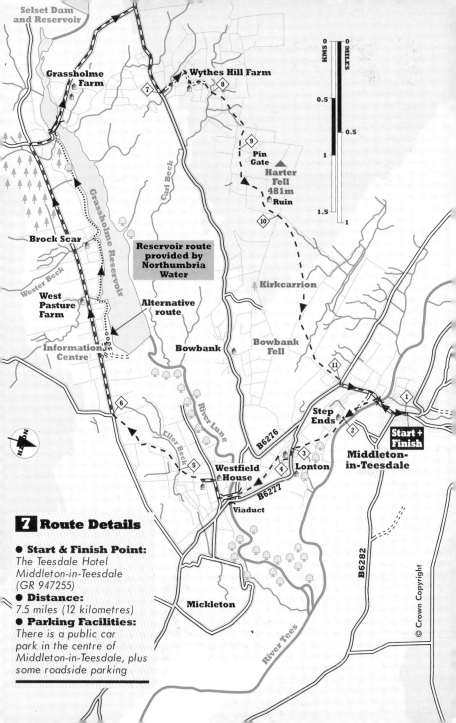

Selset Dam
and Reservoir

Grassholme
Farm

Wythes Hill Farm

7

8

Carl Beck

9

Pin
Gate

Harter Fell
481m

Ruin

10

Grassholme Reservoir

Brock Scar

Reservoir route
provided by
Northumbria
Water

Kirkcarrion

Wester Beck

West
Pasture
Farm

Alternative
route

Bowbank

Bowbank
Fell

Information
Centre

6

11

Step
Ends

1

River Lune

Eller Beck

B6276

2

Start +
Finish

NORTH

5

Westfield
House

4

3

Lonton

Middleton-
in-Teesdale

Viaduct

B6277

B6282

© Crown Copyright

7 Route Details

● **Start & Finish Point:**
*The Teesdale Hotel
Middleton-in-Teesdale
(GR 947255)*
● **Distance:**
7.5 miles (12 kilometres)
● **Parking Facilities:**
*There is a public car
park in the centre of
Middleton-in-Teesdale, plus
some roadside parking*

Mickleton

River Tees

KMS   MILES
0   0

0.5

0.5

1

1

1.5

8 Middleton·in·Teesdale - Holwick Scars - Harter Fell Circular

1 From the Teesdale Hotel turn left, along Market Place, right, along Bridge Street, crossing the Tees. Turn right just past the cattle market to join the Pennine Way.

2 From here an easy to follow track, which becomes a path, briefly edges the Tees, goes along a lane and continues, soon to return to the river, is absolute bliss. There are many stiles to cross, but always the way is clear.

3 On reaching Scoberry Bridge cross a stile on your left, leaving the Pennine Way. Go diagonally right to a white stile, left, up the next field, bearing right to another stile. Cross the field ahead to a 'Footpath' stone, then diagonally left to cross a stile into Holwick.

4 Turn right, along the road, through a facing gate, past a dwelling and uphill to a valley on the left. Descend into it, cross the beck and climb diagonally right. Cross a small stream and continue upstream, following cairns, to a facing stile.

5 Continue, still following cairns, to a facing white stile. Keep ahead, on a clear track, cross a stream, go through a gate and turn right along a thin path which soon climbs steeply before turning left, contouring to a facing gate.

6 Follow a track, curving left to edge a gill on the right to a facing gate. Beyond it, immediately turn right along a track, descend the gill to a metal hut used by grouse shooters, where the track splits.

7 Go right, out of the gill, continuing through heather, then descending to a ruinous building. Follow the path to the right of it, into a depression, which you cross and bear left to a gate in a fence.

8 Cross a rough pasture diagonally left, go through a facing gate and take the clear track towards Wythes Hill Farm ahead, keeping close to the wall on the right. On reaching a gate in it, enter a lane.

9 Go left, along it, cross a stream, climb a field to its right-hand corner, exiting at a white stile. Cross a rough pasture diagonally left, along a meandering, dipping and climbing path, to a stile on the right. Follow a broad path and, at a cairn, go left, along a farm track, through a gateway.

10 Continue right, as directed, bearing left to a facing gate, cross the field ahead, then the next one, along a track that curves left, exiting at a facing gate. Cross the field ahead on a clear track to a facing stile. Continue along a clear track through a waymarked gate, then right, to a white stile beyond which you cross the next field. Go through a gateway on your left and down the next field on a clear path to a facing gate.

11 Bear diagonally right along a clear, descending path to a gate in a fence on the left. Beyond it, bear right, over pasture to a facing gate.

12 Descend the field ahead, along a track, to the road. Turn right to the junction, then left, along the B6277, back to the start.

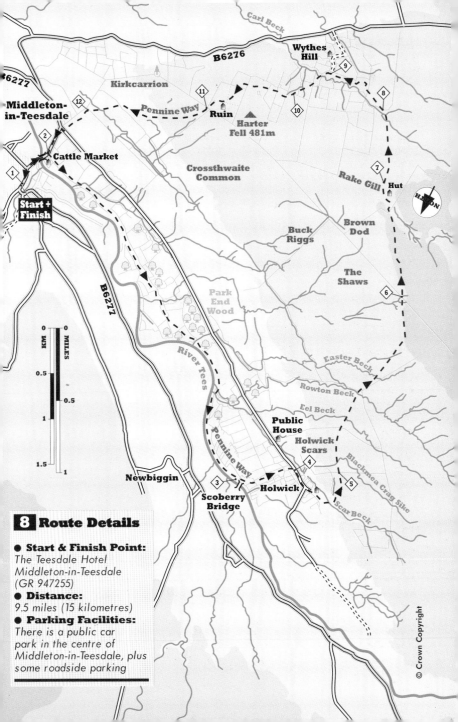

Middleton-in-Teesdale

Carl Beck

B6276

Wythes Hill

Kirkcarrion

Pennine Way

Ruin

Harter Fell 481m

Crossthwaite Common

Rake Gill

Hut

Cattle Market

Buck Riggs

Brown Dod

The Shaws

Start + Finish

B6277

Park End Wood

River Tees

Easter Beck

Rowton Beck

Eel Beck

Public House

Holwick Scars

Pennine Way

Blackmea Crag Sike

Newbiggin

Scoberry Bridge

Holwick

Scar Beck

8 Route Details

● **Start & Finish Point:**
*The Teesdale Hotel
Middleton-in-Teesdale
(GR 947255)*

● **Distance:**
9.5 miles (15 kilometres)

● **Parking Facilities:**
*There is a public car
park in the centre of
Middleton-in-Teesdale, plus
some roadside parking*

KM · MILES
0
0.5
0.5
1
1.5
1

© Crown Copyright

9 Middleton-in-Teesdale - Wynch Bridge Circular

THIS WALK AND WALK 13 CAN BE COMBINED TO CREATE A MIDDLETON-IN-TEESDALE TO HIGH FORCE CIRCULAR WALK

1 From the Teesdale Hotel cross the road and turn right along the B6277, bridge Hudeshope Beck and leave the B6277, which curves left, going straight ahead, uphill, passing, on its brow, Middleton House.

2 Continue along this quiet road, climbing steeply then pleasantly contouring the valley side. After almost a mile, Middle Side Farm is passed and the road climbs, then levels.

3 A third of a mile further on go through a gate in the wall on the left, just short of a step in it. Follow a farm track that descends to dilapidated Stonygill Head Farm, dated 1719. The track curves left, between buildings, and continues downhill, through a gateway, going diagonally right down the field ahead, through a gateway and across the next field, where it curves right to a Dutch barn. Here keep straight ahead, to cross a stile in the field's right-hand corner. The stile is awkward and care is needed here.

Go diagonally left, down the next field, to a facing gateway and keep in the same direction to a gate in a facing wall.

4 Turn right, along the B6277, and, in about 150 metres, turn left at a footpath sign into a wood. Continue along a path, fallen away in parts and hampered with fallen branches, crossing a beck on a plank bridge, nudging towards the river, through trees. Exit at a stile in a facing fence and continue up the riverside with Low Houses Farm seen on your right.

Stay on the riverbank for a good mile, crossing stiles and little streams as they appear, edging the fields and enjoying the clean air.

5 On reaching Bow Lee Beck, do not cross it at the footbridge near its confluence. Instead, bear right, along it, and cross another nearby bridge, go forward, briefly, to exit woodland and turn right, through a gate and along a grassy track, edging woodland on the right. Go through a gate to the left of a building and cross the field ahead, diagonally left, towards a beck and bear right, along it to the field corner where you turn left over it to cross a facing stile into woodland. Immediately turn right to exit over a facing stile. Edge the field ahead, close to the wall on the right, exit through a facing wicket and continue across the field ahead, close to the wall on the right. Soon to reach a kissing-gate.

6 For the more energetic, a detour extension to the route is possible. (Bear right through the gate and head for the Bowlees Visitor Centre which you can see in front of you. From here there is a pleasant walk to Gibson's Cave and Summerhill Force.) To continue our walk route turn left, across a field path, to enter woodland through a stile. Take the woodland path straight ahead, to cross the Tees on the Wynch Bridge and join the Pennine Way.

7 Turn left, along a crystal clear, riverside path, downstream, for an exhilarating return to Middleton guided by easily seen yellow arrows. Where the river loops, the path takes a more direct route, but is easy to follow and never strays very far.

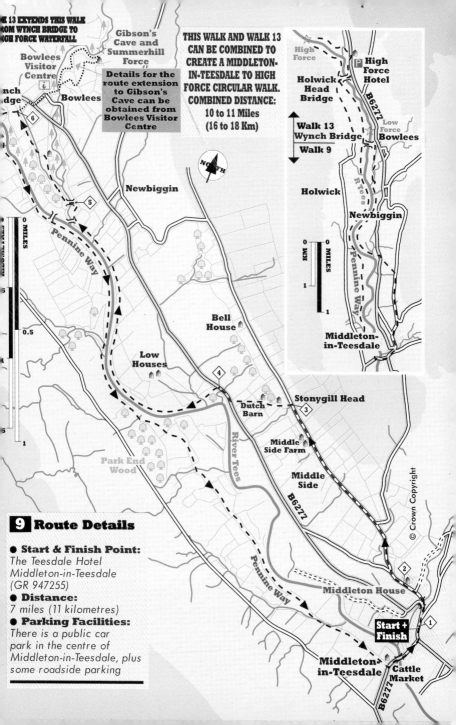

WALK 13 EXTENDS THIS WALK FROM WYNCH BRIDGE TO HIGH FORCE WATERFALL

Gibson's Cave and Summerhill Force

Bowlees Visitor Centre

Bowlees

Wynch Bridge

Details for the route extension to Gibson's Cave can be obtained from Bowlees Visitor Centre

THIS WALK AND WALK 13 CAN BE COMBINED TO CREATE A MIDDLETON-IN-TEESDALE TO HIGH FORCE CIRCULAR WALK. COMBINED DISTANCE: 10 to 11 Miles (16 to 18 Km)

High Force

High Force Hotel

Holwick Head Bridge

B6277

Low Force

Bowlees

Walk 13 Wynch Bridge

Walk 9

Holwick

Newbiggin

R Tees

Pennine Way

0 KM

0 MILES

1

1

Middleton-in-Teesdale

NORTH

Newbiggin

Pennine Way

0 MILES

0.5

1

Bell House

Low Houses

4

Stonygill Head

3

Dutch Barn

Middle Side Farm

Middle Side

B6277

River Tees

Park End Wood

© Crown Copyright

9 Route Details

● **Start & Finish Point:**
The Teesdale Hotel Middleton-in-Teesdale (GR 947255)
● **Distance:**
7 miles (11 kilometres)
● **Parking Facilities:**
There is a public car park in the centre of Middleton-in-Teesdale, plus some roadside parking

Pennine Way

Middleton House

2

1

Start + Finish

Middleton-in-Teesdale

Cattle Market

B6277

Middleton-in-Teesdale - Snaisgill - Beck Road - River Tees Circular

1 From the Teesdale Hotel go left, through the town.

2 Just beyond the last building on the left, turn left, over a set back stile and immediately turn right, up the field, aiming for a stile in a section of wall ahead. Edge the next field and, where the fence becomes a wall that curves left, do likewise to exit at a corner stile alongside a gate.

3 Go diagonally left, leaving the field at a stile near its right-hand corner. Edge the field ahead to a right-hand corner stile and immediately turn left, along a short lane. Continue close to a wall on your left and go under a facing arch. Continue uphill, bearing right, and go through a facing gate, where turn right, along a climbing track, close to a wall on the right. When the track curves left, keep alongside the wall, to a facing stile. Cross the rough pasture ahead, still close to the right-hand wall, and exit at a facing waymarked stile.

4 Cross the road, diagonally left, to a signposted stile and continue diagonally left, up the field ahead, to cross a stile in the left-hand wall, short of a farm building. Cross the next field diagonally right, exiting over a facing stile about 20 metres left of the right-hand corner. Go diagonally right over the next field to a facing stile a few metres beyond the foundations of a wall. Continue diagonally right, down the next field, leaving through a stile in a wall on the right, near the field corner and cross the next field diagonally left, to a stile mid-way along the wall on your left. Continue diagonally right, across another field, exit through a stile about ¾ of the way down the wall on your right and immediately turn left, to exit at a facing left-hand corner stile. Cross the next field, diagonally right and leave at a signposted stile, to the left of a house.

5 Turn right along a minor road which soon curves left around the head of Snaisgill and turn left at the end of the plantation on your left, as signposted. Follow a pleasant path just inside its edge, which turns right and descends to Hudeshope Beck.

6 Turn left along a tarmac road and, on reaching a bridge over Hudeshope Beck on the right, leave the road and turn right, over it.

7 Follow a clear, climbing track and on approaching a facing house, go left, along a path, fronting, then going between houses, entering Middleton down some steps.

8 Cross the road, diagonally right, to follow a path to the B6277. Turn left, along it then first right just past the old school along a lane that soon curves right and narrows. Follow it to its end. Continue, briefly, along a track and where the wall on the left ends, turn left to the riverside.

9 Take the riverside path downstream, crossing Hudeshope Beck, then the road to the left of the bridge over the Tees.

10 Follow another riverside path to a water flow gauging station, turn left and where the road splits, turn left again.

11 Walk under an arch and turn left at the main road through Middleton to the Teesdale Hotel.

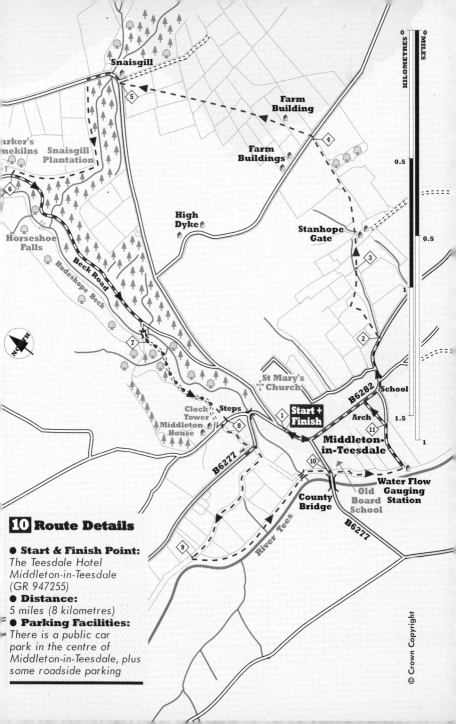

Snaisgill

Farm
Building

5

4

Barker's
Limekilns

Snaisgill
Plantation

6

Farm
Buildings

Stanhope
Gate

3

Horseshoe
Falls

High
Dyke

Beck Road

Hudeshope Beck

2

NORTH

7

St Mary's
Church

School

B6282

1

Start +
Finish

Clock
Tower
Middleton
House

Steps

8

Arch

11

Middleton-
in-Teesdale

10

B6277

Water Flow
Gauging
Station

County
Bridge

Old
Board
School

River Tees

9

B6277

KILOMETRES

MILES

0.5

0.5

1

1.5

1

1

10 **Route Details**

● **Start & Finish Point:**
*The Teesdale Hotel
Middleton-in-Teesdale
(GR 947255)*
● **Distance:**
5 miles (8 kilometres)
● **Parking Facilities:**
*There is a public car
park in the centre of
Middleton-in-Teesdale, plus
some roadside parking*

11 Middleton-in-Teesdale - Egglesburn Chapel - River Tees Circular

1 From the Teesdale Hotel turn left, along Market Place, leaving Middleton along the B6282.

2 After almost ½ mile turn left, opposite White Gate, climbing up a steep lane. Where it curves left, turn right following a public footpath paralleling the farm track to Spring Hill. Go right, between houses, through a gate, and bear left, through another gate.

3 Briefly follow a climbing path, which quickly curves left. Almost at once turn right, up a steep, stepped path, close to the wall on the right, cross a facing stile and continue up the field ahead, exiting onto the Middleton to Stanhope road.

4 Turn right, along it, for about a mile, passing Stotley Grange, to a footpath sign some 200 metres short of a dwelling where you turn right and descend a rough pasture, leaving through a wicket gate at the left-hand corner of a facing wall.

5 Continue across rough pasture, bearing right, aiming to the right of the hillock ahead, soon to join a broad, green path which curves left at a facing wall, descending, close to the wall on the right. Just past a step in it, turn right, cross a stream on a culvert, and go through a facing gate.

Continue along a green track across the field ahead, passing a ruin on the right, contour Hempstone Knoll on your left and go through a facing gate.

6 Follow the track downhill, alongside a wall on the left, leaving through a gate to the left of a facing wall. Take a clear track, soon to cross a stream, and immediately turn right, up a bank, to a green track and turn right, along it, upstream. Go through a facing stile and cross the field ahead, edging the stream, exiting at a stile. Continue up the next field to a facing wall and turn left, alongside it, passing a farmhouse on the right, to cross a stile in the wall close to the field corner.

7 Immediately turn left along the farm road, go through a facing gate and turn left along a descending lane. Turn right at the lane end, passing Egglesburn Baptist Chapel on the corner and on reaching the B6282 cross it to join the Teesdale Way, symbolised by a dipper.

8 Go along a short lane, passing a farm on the left, and continue along a concrete road, descending towards the Tees.

9 Where the road curves left, keep straight ahead, contouring, guided by a 'Teesdale Way' sign.

Following 'Teesdale Way' signs, continue upstream along an interesting and easy to follow route that keeps close to the river throughout.

10 When the path comes down towards a caravan site on the right, cross a waymarked stile and continue straight ahead, into the field containing the caravans, leaving over a stile. Continue a little way along the next field to where the river bends, and turn right to the right-hand corner of the field, to the left of the farmhouse, leaving through a gate on the right.

11 Follow the farm lane, left, which leads you pleasantly back to the start in Middleton-in-Teesdale.

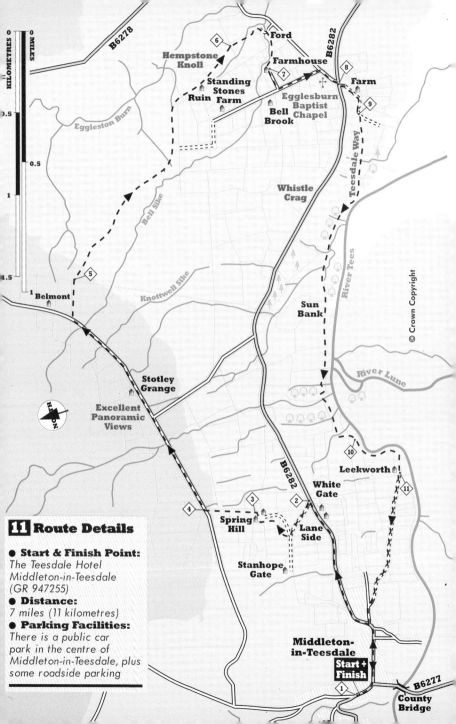

KILOMETRES
0
0 MILES

0.5

0.5

1

1.5

1

B6278

Hempstone Knoll

6

Ford

Farmhouse

7

B6282

Farm

8

9

Standing Stones Farm

Ruin

Egglesburn Baptist Chapel

Bell Brook

Eggleston Burn

Bell Sike

Whistle Crag

Teesdale Way

River Tees

© Crown Copyright

5

Belmont

Knottwell Sike

Sun Bank

River Lune

Stotley Grange

Excellent Panoramic Views

NORTH

10

Leekworth

11

B6282

White Gate

4

3

2

Spring Hill

Lane Side

Stanhope Gate

11 Route Details

● **Start & Finish Point:**
The Teesdale Hotel
Middleton-in-Teesdale
(GR 947255)

● **Distance:**
7 miles (11 kilometres)

● **Parking Facilities:**
There is a public car
park in the centre of
Middleton-in-Teesdale, plus
some roadside parking

Middleton-in-Teesdale

Start + Finish

B6277

1

County Bridge

12 The Historic Middleton-in-Teesdale Town Trail

1 From the Teesdale Hotel turn left, along Market Place, passing on your right, the Raby Estate office. Originally built as the Mechanic's Institute with financial help from the London Lead Company, it later became the Town Hall. In 1815 the London Lead Company established its northern headquarters in Middleton, which became a boom town. By 1857 nine out of ten locals were connected with the Lead industry. In 1875, Lead Company employees collected £262.15s.6d towards a retirement present for the Company's Superintendent, well in excess of what was needed. The surplus was used to purchase the handsome fountain standing at the west end of Horsemarket.

With the Methodist Chapel (1870), the Old Wesleyan Chapel (1809) and the Old Primitive Methodist Chapel (1872) all fronted by Horsemarket, the town's strong chapel connections are prominent. Set back, behind the Old Free School is more evidence: the site of an older Primitive Methodist Chapel; and at the eastern end of Horsemarket lies Chapel Row.

2 A traditional dale's farmhouse stands on Chapel Row; opposite it, go under a distinctive ornamental arch, one of about thirty built by the lead miners.

3 Continue under it, between houses, into that part of the 'new town' called Masterman Place and down to the river. The large houses with stables, on the right, just under the arch, were for under managers, surveyors and the doctor. The terraces, lower down, housed more lowly employees; and all who lived in the Company houses had to be hard working and sober.

4 Retrace your steps from the riverside water flow gauging station to where the road divides where you go right, passing Masterman Place on the left.

5 Cross the B6282 diagonally right and, short of California Row, turn left, along a pleasant back way for an off-beat view of Middleton.

6 St Mary's Church, to the right on entering Market Place, has the only detached bell tower in the Durham diocese and Richard Watson, the Teesdale poet is buried in the churchyard. Also you can see the remains of the east window from the C13th Church.

7 Bear right, past the worn stump of the Market Cross and the remains of stocks, on the right, and an old corn mill on the left, cross Hudeshope Beck and climb through Hude to Middleton House, built in 1840, passing the Clock Tower and the Lead Yard en route. The London Lead Company conducted its northern operations from Middleton House.

8 Turning left, along a path, an old Baptist Chapel (1827) and the former C17th inn, the Rose and Crown, are passed on the left and a tall sequoia dominates the parkland on the right.

9 Cross the B6277, go left, briefly, then right, along a lane, bearing left at a bend, along a walled path.

10 At its end cross Hudeshope Beck and follow a riverside path to the nearby County Bridge.

11 Turn left to reach the end of your walk.

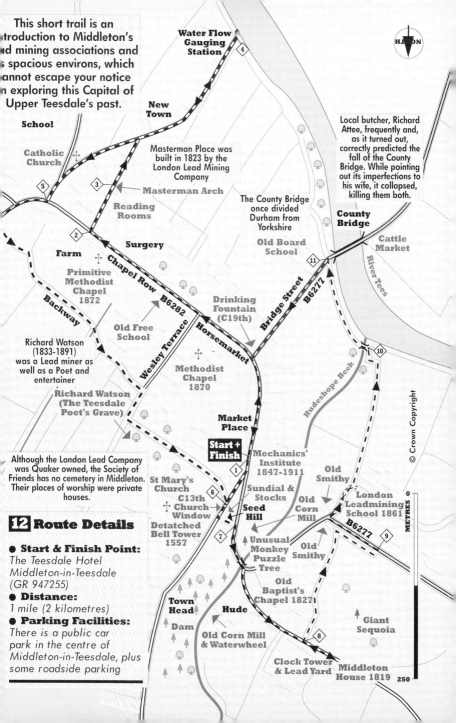

This short trail is an introduction to Middleton's lead mining associations and its spacious environs, which cannot escape your notice in exploring this Capital of Upper Teesdale's past.

Water Flow Gauging Station

4

New Town

School

Catholic Church

5

3

Masterman Arch

Masterman Place was built in 1823 by the London Lead Mining Company

Reading Rooms

Local butcher, Richard Attee, frequently and, as it turned out, correctly predicted the fall of the County Bridge. While pointing out its imperfections to his wife, it collapsed, killing them both.

The County Bridge once divided Durham from Yorkshire

County Bridge

Cattle Market

River Tees

2

Surgery

Farm

Chapel Row

Old Board School

11

B6272

Primitive Methodist Chapel 1872

B6282

Drinking Fountain (C19th)

Bridge Street

Backway

Old Free School

Wesley Terrace

Horsemarket

Richard Watson (1833-1891) was a Lead miner as well as a Poet and entertainer

Methodist Chapel 1870

Hudeshope Beck

10

Richard Watson (The Teesdale Poet's Grave)

© Crown Copyright

Market Place

Although the London Lead Company was Quaker owned, the Society of Friends has no cemetery in Middleton. Their places of worship were private houses.

Start + Finish

1

Mechanics' Institute 1847-1911

Old Smithy

London Leadmining School 1861

St Mary's Church

6

Sundial & Stocks

Old Corn Mill

B6277

9

12 **Route Details**

C13th Church Window

Seed Hill

METRES 0

Detached Bell Tower 1557

7

Old Smithy

● **Start & Finish Point:**
The Teesdale Hotel Middleton-in-Teesdale (GR 947255)

Unusual Monkey Puzzle Tree

Old Baptist's Chapel 1827

● **Distance:**
1 mile (2 kilometres)

Town Head

Hude

Giant Sequoia

● **Parking Facilities:**
There is a public car park in the centre of Middleton-in-Teesdale, plus some roadside parking

Dam

Old Corn Mill & Waterwheel

8

Clock Tower & Lead Yard

Middleton House 1819

250

13 Wynch Bridge - High Force Circular

THIS WALK AND WALK 9 CAN BE COMBINED TO CREATE A MIDDLETON-IN-TEESDALE TO HIGH FORCE CIRCULAR WALK

1 From Wynch Bridge follow the delightful riverside path for one mile to lead you to Holwick Head Bridge. Cross it, go diagonally left to the bottom of a steep wooded embankment, ascending it carefully with the help of some steps to the B6277.

2 Here turn left for 20 metres to the entrance of the High Force Waterfall Walk where a fee is payable. Follow the prepared pathway through the beautiful woods and gorge to experience the breathtaking spectacle of High Force, England's largest waterfall.

3 Returning along the path to the Waterfall Walk entrance, turn right along the B6277 for about 20 metres, where turn right as signposted. Descent a steep wooded embankment, down steps, exiting at a riverside field. Go diagonally left, across it, to Holwick Head Bridge, which you cross to join the Pennine Way.

4 Here you can retrace your riverside route to Wynch Bridge or for another unforgettable view of High Force from the opposite side of the gorge, immediately turn right and climb a stepped path to enter a National Nature Reserve. Go through it, along a clear path, upstream, to High Force.

5 From High Force, retrace your steps to leave the Nature Reserve the way you came in. Go forward briefly, and where the path splits do not take the one going straight ahead because this is not a right of way. Instead, follow the stepped path towards Holwick Head Bridge. You can either retrace your steps from the bridge along the riverside walk to Wynch Bridge or, just short of it, turn right, uphill, along a clear track, and where it curves right, in front of a dwelling, bear left along a green track to a facing gate.

6 Cross the field ahead on the green track, leaving through the right-hand of two gateways in a facing wall, traverse the next pasture close to the wall on the left, go through a facing gate and continue along the track. Go through a facing metal gate on approaching Hield House Farm.

7 Keeping to the left of the farm building, go through a second metal gate. Exit the farmyard along a farm road, walled at first and always easy to follow.

8 After passing through a metal farm gate with the tarmac road just ahead, continue towards it on the farm track to just beyond where it bridges a beck and turn left, directed by a yellow arrow on a post. Join the farm track, clearly seen ahead and bear left, along it. Soon a waymarked facing gate is reached, which you go through and continue straight ahead, directed by a yellow arrow, still on the same track, which leads to a long disused farmhouse.

9 On reaching a gateway at the side of the house do not go through it. Instead, bear left, as waymarked, alongside a wall on your right, soon to bridge the beck previously crossed. Now turn right, as waymarked, down the field and where it narrows almost to lane dimensions, turn right along it, as waymarked, and exit over a step stile. Bear slightly left, past a post carrying a yellow arrow, and go straight across the field ahead to return to Wynch Bridge.

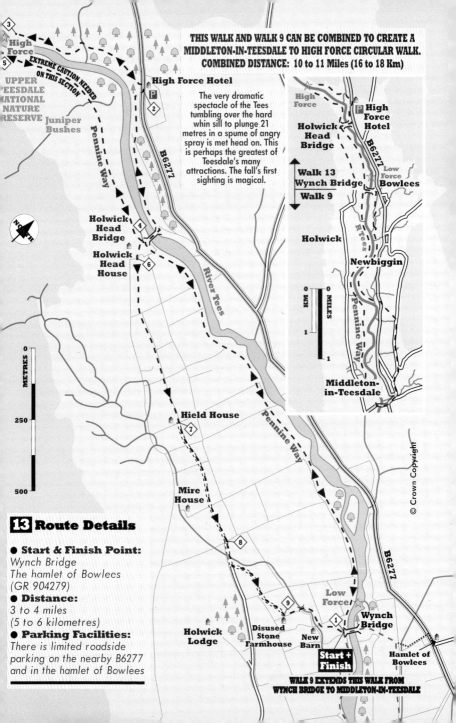

THIS WALK AND WALK 9 CAN BE COMBINED TO CREATE A MIDDLETON-IN-TEESDALE TO HIGH FORCE CIRCULAR WALK. COMBINED DISTANCE: 10 to 11 Miles (16 to 18 Km)

The very dramatic spectacle of the Tees tumbling over the hard whin sill to plunge 21 metres in a spume of angry spray is met head on. This is perhaps the greatest of Teesdale's many attractions. The fall's first sighting is magical.

EXTREME CAUTION NEEDED ON THIS SECTION

High Force

UPPER TEESDALE NATIONAL NATURE RESERVE

Juniper Bushes

High Force Hotel

Pennine Way

B6277

Holwick Head Bridge

Holwick Head House

River Tees

NORTH

Walk 13 Wynch Bridge Walk 9

High Force

High Force Hotel

Holwick Head Bridge

Low Force

Bowlees

R. Tees

Holwick

Newbiggin

Pennine Way

Middleton-in-Teesdale

© Crown Copyright

KM 0 / MILES 0

1 / 1

METRES
0
250
500

Hield House

Mire House

Pennine Way

13 Route Details

● **Start & Finish Point:**
Wynch Bridge
The hamlet of Bowlees
(GR 904279)
● **Distance:**
3 to 4 miles
(5 to 6 kilometres)
● **Parking Facilities:**
There is limited roadside parking on the nearby B6277 and in the hamlet of Bowlees

Holwick Lodge

Disused Stone Farmhouse

New Barn

Low Force

Wynch Bridge

Hamlet of Bowlees

Start + Finish

WALK 9 EXTENDS THIS WALK FROM WYNCH BRIDGE TO MIDDLETON-IN-TEESDALE

WALKING AND SAFETY TIPS

This section is virtually the same as we publish in our Walks of Discovery Series which is designed for the very serious walker covering much longer routes on very difficult and high altitude terrain. However, the basic principles still apply so we have retained this detail for your information.

It is absolutely essential that anyone venturing out into the countryside, particularly hilly terrain, be correctly prepared to reduce the risk of injury or fatality. No amount of advice could cover all possible situations that may arise. Therefore the following walking and safety tips are not intended to be an exhaustive list, but merely a contribution from our personal experiences for your consideration.

Clothing & Equipment

The lists represent the basic equipment required to enjoy a full day's hill walking, reasonably safe and comfortably.

CLOTHING:- Strong, sensible footwear - preferably boots with a good sole, strong trainers or lightweight boots can be worn during prolonged dry weather, warm shirt, fibre pile jacket, warm woollen sweater, windproof and waterproof anorak with hood and leggings (several thin layers insulate more adequately than one layer), woollen gloves, woollen hat or balaclava, warm trousers (avoid denim/jeans which become very clammy and cold when wet. This could lead to exposure), and good quality woollen socks or stockings, protected by waterproof gaiters.

EQUIPMENT:- Good compass and maps of the areas, along with a survival bag, whistle or torch for implementing the International Distress Signal - 6 long blasts/flashes in quick succession followed by one minute pause then repeated (the answering signal is 3 blasts or flashes). A basic first aid kit should also be carried, which contains - bandages, sticking plasters, safety pins, scissors and some gauze pads. Take a rucksack to carry your equipment in, and some food for a butty stop, plus some extra food for emergency rations - chocolate, fruit cake, cheese and dried fruit.

Preparation & Procedure

Ensure that yourself and the others are adequately equipped and that no-one is overburdened. Learn how to use your map and compass competently. You should always be able to at least locate yourself on a map. Find out the weather forecasts for the area. Always consider the wind chill factor - even the gentlest of winds can reduce effective temperatures to a dangerous level. Plan both the route and possible escape routes beforehand balancing terrain, weather forecast and the hours of daylight against experience whilst allowing for a safety margin. Always try to plan your walk so the prevailing wind is behind you. Always try to walk in company. It is safer and more enjoyable.